Books by Buff Whitman-Bradley

Poetry
b. eagle, poet
The Honey Philosophies
At the Driveway Guitar Sale
The Heron Could Be Lost
And What Will We Sing?

Nonfiction
Growing From Word Play Into Poetry
Endings: A Book About Death
Where Do I Belong? A Kids' Guide to Stepfamilies
About Face: Military Resisters Turn Against War (ed.)

A FRIENDLY LITTLE TAVERN SOMEWHERE NEAR THE PLEIADES

poems by

Buff Whitman-Bradley

Finishing Line Press
Georgetown, Kentucky

A FRIENDLY LITTLE TAVERN SOMEWHERE NEAR THE PLEIADES

Copyright © 2024 by Buff Whitman-Bradley
ISBN 979-8-88838-791-7 First Edition
All rights reserved under International and Pan-American Copyright Conventions. No part of this book may be reproduced in any manner whatsoever without written permission from the publisher, except in the case of brief quotations embodied in critical articles and reviews.

Publisher: Leah Huete de Maines
Editor: Christen Kincaid
Cover Art: Painting: *Tavern Scene,* 1827. Johann Baptist Pflug (1785-1866). Public Domain
Author Photo: Nina Norgeot
Cover Design: Elizabeth Maines McCleavy

Order online: www.finishinglinepress.com
also available on amazon.com

Author inquiries and mail orders:
Finishing Line Press
PO Box 1626
Georgetown, Kentucky 40324
USA

Contents

Ants 1
Birthday poem 3
Three hawks 4
Growing old 5
A cold, gray day 7
Now comes pale dusk 8
Bishop Woodpecker 10
Goodnight Earth 11
Roadside grasses 13
Summer jobs 14
Our place 15
Heat wave 16
The blackberries of August 17
Lucky stars 18
COVID booster 20
A bit plonky 23
Almost out loud 24
Existential blues 25
The Big Tomato 27
Winter solstice 28
All will be well 30
Frog songs 31
Morning hawk 33
Tomorrow's grasses 34
All day the cows 35
Decline 37
Somewhere near the Pleiades 40
Not to be confused with scribbling 41

Reading to the dog	42
My new Swiss Army knife	43
Beside themselves	44
What happened	45
We do not identify flowers	48
Thanksgiving Eve	49
Another memorable performance	50
My 80th spring	51
About me	53
#2 pencil	55
Mail	57
If I were in charge	58
After a long pause	59
Winter night	60
A day in November	61
Falling down in five chapters	63
Gray, somber day	66
Cote d'Azur	67
Merit badges	68
Clouds of memory	70
Old poets	71
Life is different in your eighties	73
Masterpiece	74
Sadness	76
Something wonderful	77
Your name	78
After his funeral	79
Just now an ant	80
Acknowledgments	82
About the author	83

For Roger Stoll

Ants

At night
When the ants
Bring their final loads of the day
Back to the communal space
And close the entrance
Behind them,
Leaving a few outside
To guard against
Invasion and mayhem,
Before they retire
For the evening
They form into small groups
To discuss large questions,
For example
What is the size of the soul?
There are various points of view:
Some say the size of the soul
Is relative
To the size of the body—
The larger the creature, the larger the soul.
Others contend
That the soul of an ant
Is exactly the same size
As the souls of the huge, heavy-footed gods
Who walk about so gracelessly,
Crushing ants and beetles
And kindred life forms
Heedlessly and willy-nilly
Beneath their enormous, deadly
Grotesquely armored pedal appendages.
And some take the radical view
That the size of the soul
Is in inverse correlation
To the size of the body,
That the soul of an ant
Is vast,
Whereas the soul
Of those clumsy
Clomping, tromping deities

Is so miniscule
As to be virtually undetectable.
These different opinions
Are always addressed
With the utmost courtesy
For all ants admire and respect each other.
There is no arguing, no yelling,
No storming away in a huff.
And after a vigorous airing
Of everyone's ideas,
Like all of us after a long, hard day,
The ants grow tired and ready for sleep.
So they bid each other good night,
Find suitable spots
Amongst their hundreds of companions
For settling down with their souls,
And fall quickly into a sweet slumber
Of exactly the right size.

Birthday poem

This morning I took my coffee
Out to the bench in front of our house
And sat chatting with my wife and the neighbors.
Many strollers passed by
And having turned 78 today
I was feeling magnanimous and a bit papal
So I blessed each one of them
Although not out loud.
This is the oldest I have ever been
And I am pondering
The contours of my new age
Trying to make some sense
Of what it all means.
It is early yet so I have come
To no definite conclusions
But I am getting an inkling
That I have at last
Achieved a certain gravitas
And will shortly feel free
To dispense advice indiscriminately
Whether anyone asks for it
Or not.
Listen more, speak less
I will tell people I pass on the street
Or sit next to on the bus
Be patient, especially with children.
Practice large generosity.
Stay in the bike lane and
Walk your dog at least twice a day.
Think much, believe little.
Forgive.
Of course everyone already knows
All of this
But how affirming it will be
How reassuring
To hear these truths pronounced
By this kindly old gentleman
Who is so willing to share his wisdom
And who does not at all, by the way,
Look his age.

Three hawks

A sodden morning
After an all-night soaking
Here at the bottom of an atmospheric river.
The tub-thumping rains
And the pains in my leg
Kept me awake for hours
And I arose with big plans
For an early afternoon nap.
After breakfast
We walked the dog
Along the dripping streets
Where all color had been drained
Into sidewalk puddles
And overflowing gutters.
Persimmon trees
Were emptied of their ornaments.
Great piles of drenched leaves
Clogged storm drains.
The creek was drunkenly muddy
As it barreled through town
Carrying fallen tree limbs
And lost soccer balls.
The air had sharp teeth,
And the sky was a great, gray scowl.
But above the tall hillside oaks
The whistling and wheeling
Of three red-tailed hawks
Drew our gaze upwards
And lifted our spirits
On an unpromising winter day
I'd almost given up on.

Growing old

We have noticed
That growing old sometimes happens
Without notifying us.
For example,
We may make big plans
To circumambulate the Dolomites
Only to have our bones
Mumble and grumble their discontent,
Our joints threaten
To sue us for damages,
And our shoes keep filling up with rain.
And yet we carry on,
Each day doing our best
To feel grateful,
To muster up a little appreciation
For some small gift
Reminding us that, yes,
Creaky as we may be,
Here we still are,
Still paying thankful attention
To a pyracantha bush heavy
With bright red berries,
A single small puff of cloud
In the vast blueness of day,
An officious crow
Strutting like a lieutenant colonel
Around the front yard,
A pileated woodpecker
Hammering away on a redwood.

We know we have a prepaid reservation
On old Charon's rowboat,
We know our departure date
Is steadily approaching,
But on the ride across the water
We'll be happy to entertain our fellow passengers
With a tale of how,
On a rainy day in the winter woods,
We came upon a log

Entirely covered
By an exquisitely woven red and black cloth
Which turned out to be not a cloth at all
But thousands of hibernating ladybugs
Keeping each other warm,
And of how, in that shimmering instant,
We forgot to be old.

A cold, gray day

A cold, gray day promising rain.
The dog and I are staying inside.
He is sitting at one end of the couch
Staring out the front window
Alert for passersby
Both human and canine
At whom he can bark ferociously,
While I am planted at the other end,
A low table in front of me
On which there is a steaming cup
Of lemon ginger tea
Along with three books,
Poetry, novel, nonfiction.
I read from each of them,
A few pages in this one,
A paragraph or two in that one,
A short poem from the third
Then once more and once more.
I sip my tea,
Pause to pet the dog,
Look outside wondering
When the storm will begin.
There are moments in a life
When everything coalesces
In a kind of sweet equilibrium,
When the bills are paid,
And the chores are done,
When no worries nag at you,
When your back isn't hurting.
A large stillness settles over you then,
With your books and your tea and your dog,
And it occurs to you
That this might just be the best day
Anyone has ever had
And that on such a day
A person could probably live forever,
So you do.

Now comes pale dusk

Now comes pale dusk
As the sun slips behind the near hills
And long, cold shadows
Begin patrolling the streets
To hunt down
Any vagrant light and warmth
Still eluding the oncoming darkness
And the sudden drop
In temperature.

Now comes pale dusk
As anarchic flights of crows
Spread across the washed-out blue
Of the rice paper sky
Like gangs
Of fugitive calligraphy.

Now comes pale dusk
As one light after another
Flicks on in houses
Up and down the block
And loose formations
Of after-school teenagers
Carrying homework on their backs
Converse without looking up
From the illuminated screens
Of their cell phones
Yet somehow manage
To navigate their way home.

Now comes pale dusk
As skunks and racoons and possums
Begin to stir
And prepare themselves
For another graveyard shift
And owls high up in redwoods
And oaks and firs
Practice hoo-ing softly
To tune up their vocal cords
For the nightlong conversations ahead.

Now comes pale dusk
As memories permeate the hour's air
Like the aroma of woodsmoke,
As the clamorings of my regrets subside
And all my knotted sadnesses
Come quietly untied.

Bishop Woodpecker

for Gyl Bradley

Perched atop the power pole
Like an avian bishop
The pileated woodpecker
Surveys the neighborhood,
Perhaps to bless the faithful
And look with pity
Upon the unconverted.
His erect posture
And dignified mien are imposing,
His clothing impressive—
Jet black robe
Bright red miter
That mark him as one
Of substance and significance.
In the woods we often hear him
But he rarely shows himself,
So his appearance now
In our ordinary little neighborhood
Is quite the honor.
Of course like all
Who are aware of their own importance,
This bishop does not stick around
For long,
There are so many lost souls
To attend to,
So many tithes to collect,
So many dinners with influential laity.
So he utters a high, clear, piping benediction
Then abruptly flies away
Into the trees
Knowing that
If he attends faithfully
To his ecclesiastical duties
He could, one day,
Become a cardinal.

Goodnight Earth

> *(with gratitude for Margaret Wise Brown's children's classic,*
> Goodnight Moon*)*

Goodnight Earth
So small and slight
We're sad to leave
Your daytime light
And starlit nights

Goodnight Earth
We cannot say
We did our best,
Now there's no way
That we can stay

Goodnight raging forest fires
Goodnight rising seas
Goodnight melting glaciers
Goodnight honey bees
And so much more than these

Goodnight to the children
Who never breathed clean air
Who ate contaminated food
And didn't have a prayer
In a world so damned unfair

Goodnight to those who fought
For justice and equality
A turn to wiser ways
Of diversity and sanity
And universal community

Goodnight friends and loved ones
Goodnight plants and beasts
Of our sad little planet
That we've caused to overheat
And otherwise mistreat

We won't be coming back
We had our chance and blew it
Our story has a moral
But no one left to listen to it
(Or willfully misconstrue it)

So goodnight creek
Good night birds
Goodnight music
Goodnight words

Goodnight window
Goodnight door
Goodnight slippers
On the floor

Goodnight games
Goodnight toys
Goodnight girls
And goodnight boys

Goodnight chair
Goodnight spoon
Goodnight stars
And goodnight moon

Goodnight lark
And owl and thrush
Goodnight old lady
Whispering *Hush*

Goodnight Earth

Roadside grasses

Ordinarily, they are quite modest,
Live quietly,
Seek no attention,
But today
In high winds
They are putting on a show
Swaying their long, lithe, golden bodies
With unrestrained exuberance,
Waving wildly
And calling out
"Look at us! Look at us!"
To those speeding past
Along the roadway.
And we do look at them
And it is impossible not to imagine
The thrill surging
Through those slender, graceful stems
As gust after gust
Of muscular winds
Dizzy them in the dance.

Summer jobs

Five P.M., first afternoon
Of the latest heat wave.
The young couple across the street
Return from a day of work
Washing windows.
"How'd it go?" we call out to them
And they reply with the good cheer
Of the youthful
"Not too bad"
As they drag themselves up the stairs
To their apartment.
I remember the overheated work days
Of summer jobs
Loading trucks, mowing golf courses
Cleaning out freight cars
To get them ready for the next load.
I remember my work shirts
Soaked with sweat.
I remember blistering my hands
On shovel handles
And burning my unprotected back and shoulders
In the scorching sunlight.
I remember the laborers I worked with
For a couple of months each summer
For whom this job was not a break
Between semesters
But what they did to feed their families.
They were always kind to me
Always invited me for a beer
After a brutal day in the punishing sun.
And in August
As I was leaving to return to school,
To reassume the privileges
That I had never earned
And they had never had,
They always bade me farewell
With a kind of gruff tenderness—
"Stay in school, kid," they'd say,
"You don't want to be doing this
For the rest of your life."

Our place

Grains of pollen scattering invisibly
In a stiff breeze,
Bits of soil and gravel
Dislodged from the garden
And scattered on the sidewalk,
A small branch snapped off
The sycamore tree
And lying on the roof
Of the garage,
A house finch stopping momentarily
On the power line out front
Then flitting away without a note,
A butterfly wing
Snagged on the ceanothus,
Blueberries ripening quietly
In the back yard,
These and all other
Small and insignificant facts of life
That remain mostly unnoticed
Are whispered reminders of our place
In all of time
And all of space.

Heat wave

We have been warned
By the National Weather Service
And various witty and well-groomed
TV meteorologists
That a heat wave is on its way
Perhaps to settle some scores.
Good of them to let us know.
We will close our windows
And pull down the blinds
To keep out as much heat as possible,
To keep our homes as cool as possible,
But we know that in the end
These are futile gestures
And at some point in the afternoon
The thermal gunslinger will disembark
From the 3:12 to Yuma
And walk slowly along our streets
His six-guns blazing
Penetrating our meager domestic defenses
And rendering us incapable of resistance.
Drained of energy and vitality
And the will to bake chocolate chip cookies
We will sweat and slump through the day
Until evening when,
If we are lucky,
The villain will board the last train out of town
And leave us to open the windows and doors
Letting the evening breezes waft amiably
Through our houses
Erasing any reminders
Of our sweltering ordeal.
But if our karma's lousy
He will stick around,
Leaving us to sweat it out all night long
Sleepless on perspiration-soaked sheets
Dreading what diabolical
Fahrenheits and centigrades
The Death Valley Kid will torment us with
In the days ahead.

The blackberries of August

In the midst of the backyard party
I slip away
To take a walk down the road
Where I know blackberries
Are waiting.
And although I hate
The pricks and stabs
And scratches and gouges
Of their ferociously thorned
Tangles of vines,
When I see those voluptuous
Deep purple berries
Dangling there for the taking
I don't hesitate
And reach in again and again
Not oblivious, exactly,
To the repeated painful jabbings
I am experiencing
But obsessed with finding
The darkest, ripest, juiciest
Little firecrackers of sweetness
That burst on my tongue
When I pop them into my mouth,
My fingers sticky and stained with their juice,
My inner child urging me on—
"Just one more, just one more."
However, when my mature, responsible self
Decides it is time I returned
To the festivities on the lawn,
As I am heading back up the road
I notice that my arms
Are covered with little pokes and punctures
And lacerations,
Some of which are bleeding a bit
And beginning to sting.
But when it comes to gathering
The blackberries of August
Old guy and inner kid agree
That a little bloodshed
Is a small price to pay.

Lucky stars

On the front porch
As the sky darkens
And the full moon eases into place
Above the neighbor's house
We have a conversation
About the recent telescopic photos
Taken from outer space.
Astronomers explain
That the bright specks in those photos
Are galaxies
Whose light has traveled 13 billion years
To reach us.
I have no way to comprehend this.
I am numbed and dumbed
By the immensity of the universe,
By the puniness of us.
I had an old compadre who used to say
When things got difficult
He reminded himself
That in the big picture
We are merely accidental brush strokes.
He called this
His cosmic frame of reference—
You're a twitch of a gnat's eyebrow
And you'll be gone before you know it,
So figure out what really matters to you
And don't sweat the small stuff.
I'm sure for some
That mulling over our insignificance
And very brief tenure
Could be incentive to dive in
To the Slough of Despond.
On the other hand
However tinily, however temporarily we are here,
We stand in the midst of colossal, heart-pounding
Tambourine-banging, inter-galactic grandeur,
So perhaps instead of grumbling
About the terms and clauses and sub-paragraphs
Of our contract with mortality,

While we're here awaiting
The last stage out of Tombstone,
We might want to head for the top of Boot Hill
To contemplate the breathtaking splendor
Of all that is,
To lean back, look up, take a deep breath
And thank our lucky stars.

COVID booster

As the tip of the needle
Penetrated the flesh
Of my upper arm
Just millimeters from
The Kokopelli tattoo
I thought about
All the cowboy movies
I watched as a boy
In which
The simple, honest,
Humble townsfolk
Get wind of
The impending arrival
Of a gang of thugs and rapists
And murderers
Intent upon wreaking havoc
And mayhem
As retribution for the refusal
Of the mayor's beautiful daughter
To marry their malodorous boss.
Learning that the vicious crew
Is only a couple of days distant
The residents pool their meager resources
To hire a notorious gunslinger,
A good bad guy,
To protect them from
The bad bad guys on the way.
Of course, the good bad guy accepts the job
But refuses the pay
Then goes about drafting
Various other good bad guys
To assist him
In fashioning a ferocious fighting force
Out of ordinary grocers
And blacksmiths and school marms
And preachers and dance hall girls
And housewives and stage coach drivers
And wheelwrights
And even the disgraced former sheriff

Who cannot keep his booze intake
Under control.
As the approach
Of the bad bad guys
Grows ever more ominous,
Which can be readily inferred
From the award-winning soundtrack,
Composed by a Slovenian immigrant maestro
Living in splendor in the Hollywood hills,
The good bad guys
Instruct the jittery citizens
In the fine arts of riflery and six-shooting
Of building fortifications with hay bales
And bags of un-milled wheat
And overturned buckboards,
Of strategically placing
Sticks of dynamite used heretofore
Only for peaceful purposes.
The music grows darker
The sound of galloping hooves
Becomes louder and louder
And suddenly the bad bad guys
Have arrived at the edge of town
Slowing their horses to a walk
And sneering right malevolently
As they pass by the dry goods store
The Broken Heart saloon
The sheriff's empty office
The one-room school
And Old Widow McCarthy's boarding house.
Hearts beat fast and loud
Breaths are held
Fingers twitch on triggers and . . .
"That's it," said the inoculating nurse
"You're good to go."
I rolled down my sleeve
Pocketed my vaccine verification card
And headed back to my car
Confident that as always

The good bad guys
(Who, truth be known,
Aren't really bad,
Just misconstrued)
Will save the threatened town
Then head out past the Buckskin Corral
Toward parts unknown.

A bit plonky

COVID booster yesterday
Vaguely worried
About a bad reaction
But woke up this morning
Feeling pretty OK
Made breakfast
Took a walk
Got coffee
At the neighborhood joint
Sat reading in the big yellow chair.
Early afternoon started feeling
A bit plonky
A bit overbaked
Reconnoitered the bedroom
And found the sun
Sprawled invitingly
Across the bed
So what could I do
But lie down
Joined soon
By the little dog
Who concurred with me
About the existential imperative
Of a sunny nap.
So we had a fine old snooze
Awoke then
Heated some soup
Cut up an apple
Boiled water for a cup
Of peppermint tea
Steaming in a mug now
On the table
Beside the big yellow chair
To which I have returned
With nothing to do
But sit and sip
And read a book
With a lapful of warm dog.

Almost out loud

Every spring
The large ceanothus plant
In our front yard blooms
Almost out loud
Hundreds of tiny blue brushes
Kicking up such a rip-roaring rumpus
That bees from miles around
Come racing to see
What's going on.
And when they arrive
They become instantly intoxicated
By a subtly seductive
Lilac perfume
Which sends them into euphoric fits
Of nonstop nectaring
All the daylight hours
Making endless trips back and forth
Between shrub and hive
As happy carriers of fresh sustenance
For the whole buzzing community.
Then as night comes down
Out of the hills
The bees make one last visit
To that abundant font
Of sweet elixir
Before heading to the bunkhouse
Where they will dream
The entire night long
Of tomorrow's gathering spree
While,
Embraced by darkness,
The fragrant shrub
Will spend the dreaming hours
Stirring up batch after batch of nectar
For, unlike those tuckered out apian toilers,
The wildly awake ceanothus,
Having spent the winter in a doze,
Has no intention of nodding off now.

Existential blues

This is my 79th spring
And I am thinking two thoughts
At once:
How lucky I have been
To be present 79 times
For this seasonal return
To vivid, abundant vitality; and
Whoa! Slow down! I'm not ready for this!
I have been reading
The poems of T'ao Ch'ien
Full of laments
About the passing of all things
Including us
But also brimming with delight
At the beauty in which
We are allowed to participate
For the short while
That we are here.
Depending on which moment
You catch me
I might be celebrating
The flowering quince down the street
The brand-new milkmaids
And hounds tongues in the woods
The hawks high above us
Screeching for love.
Or I could be mired
In the Bog of Despair
Stewing about the fact
That my days are numbered
And the number keeps growing smaller
And smaller.
Right at this moment
I am sitting in the overstuffed rocker
In the front room,
Sun pouring in through the picture window,
Watching our granddaughter
Play with her new doll house
And construct elaborate and ever-shifting narratives

For the inhabitants
Both human and non—
Horses in the bathtub
A giraffe cooking breakfast
A shiny little boy and girl riding bikes
On the stairway
Furniture soaring up to the roof
A bright yellow bear
Leaping through a window
A magic rabbit
Turning the whole gang
Into parrots
Who then fly off to Africa—
And it occurs to me
That whenever the existential blues
Come upon me
I've just got to stop moping about mortality
Embrace the impermanence of everything
Everywhere
Ever
Then get myself down on the floor
To play with some unicorns.

The Big Tomato

We ought to have let ourselves
Feel awed
By the vastness in which
We are the merest flecks

We ought to have allowed ourselves
To be grateful
For the millions of years
Of microbial bumper-carring
That made it possible
Quite by happy accident
For us to become us

We should have been satisfied
To be a-swim with all the other ingredients
In the great cosmic chowder
Instead of acting like the Big Tomato
And threatening to capsize the whole tureen

And now here we are
Neck deep in hubris
The soup rising all around us
As urgently we rummage
Through the pantry
And the crisper drawer
For all the organic
Sustainably produced, carbon-neutral
Eco-friendly ingredients
We can use to whip up
A mouth-watering
And very virtuous gazpacho
To enchant the palate
And save the planet

Winter solstice

As the sun glides down
Behind the far hills
Pulling the sky's bright blue counterpane
Along with it
Dark begins to come out of hiding
From the low places
Where mushrooms hunker
And cold bides its time.

Kids race home on their bikes
With night following close behind,
And gaining.
Rumors of moonrise
Begin to circulate
Among the nocturnal crowd—
Owls, coyotes, possums, skunks.
The crepusculars
Grab what morsels they can
In the fading light
And the heliotropic among us
Start flicking on house lights
And holiday lights
Up and down the block.

This is the season of long nights
When we scan the icy
Star-filled blackness
For the pure pleasure
Of glimpsing old friends—
Orion, Cassiopeia, the Pleiades—
When we are reminded
By two trillion galaxies
That our existence is infinitesimal,
Of no cosmic significance,
And when we realize all over again
That what we call grace
Is not a celestial gift
Showered down upon us
From skies beyond the sky,

But a quality within each of us,
A soft ticking in the cells,
A whisper in the blood.

All will be well

I wake every night
For an hour or so
Go to the living room with a book
Or a crossword puzzle
Stay up long enough
For the pains in my leg
To subside
Then head back to bed.
It can be lonely
In the solitary stillness of 2 A.M.
And sometimes,
To keep me company,
My froggy old brain
Begins to fuss and fret
About matters both significant
And trivial.
But when I hear the owls
Calling to each other
From the large oaks
Down the street
Even though I know
They are not talking to me
I feel soothed and comforted
As I did when I was a child
Lying curled up and barely awake
In the back of the car
While my parents chatted quietly
In the front seat
And I listened not to their words
But to the sounds of their voices,
A soft blanket of talk
Wrapped around a little boy
As he drifted off to sleep,
Assuring him that all will be well
And all will be well.

Frog songs

In the marsh
The frogs are unperturbed
By the cold, wet weather.
Quite to the contrary
They are celebrating
With songs of jubilation,
Choruses of alleluias,
Joyous cantatas
Of incomparable beauty
That continue hour after hour
Even as the rains
Pelt the murky standing waters,
The large patches of mud,
The matted reeds and grasses.

In the marsh
The frog songs rise
Up through the nearby trees
All the way to amphibian heaven
Where all frogs
From the immemorial past
Sit quietly in ethereal muck
Listening to the primeval tunes
That they themselves sang
When it was their time,
Their turn,
To bless the world with the music
Only they could make.

In the marsh
As night rises
Out of the murky standing waters,
The large patches of mud,
The matted reeds and grasses,
Little by little the darkening sky
Embraces the melodies and harmonies
Of ancient and holy frog music,
Finds a place in the firmament
For each and every note,

And each and every note
Becomes a star.

Morning hawk

This morning as I was warming up
To do the daily stretches
That help keep me from
Becoming cemented in place
I looked out the window and spotted
A small, handsome hawk
With dark wings
And a pale, barred breast
Perched on a fencepost
Behind the tool shed.
I'm no hawkster
So I can't tell you the name
Of that backyard visitor
But what I can tell you
Is that catching sight
Of that splendid bird
In a moment of pause—
Hers and mine—
Lifted my spirits immeasurably,
Filled me with enthusiasm
For the day ahead,
Reminded me that we inhabit
A universe of small wonders
As well as large ones,
Caused me to blurt out a prayer
To all that is:
"O, Infinite and Eternal Cosmos,
Just wanted to thank you
For the hawk sighting.
You probably don't know who I am,
But I've been watching you work
For decades
And I'm a big fan.
Amen."

Tomorrow's grasses

Two horses are grazing
In a broad field of winter grasses.
One of the horses is a chestnut
The other is dark brown.
They are standing far apart
From each other.
The air is cold and damp.
The sky is growing dark.
Neither horse seems in a hurry
To finish eating
And head back to the stables
At the close of day.
The trees at the edge of the field
Have lost all their leaves.
With their limbs bared
They look quite formidable.
They might be sentries
Guarding a nighttime bivouac
Making certain no unwanted intruders
Cross the perimeter.
The horses seem to trust them
To be vigilant
Allowing them to continue grazing
Without fear of interruption
By coyotes or wolves.
Soon it will be completely night.
The difference in color
Of the two horses
Is gradually disappearing.
They will become dusky shapes
Walking slowly through the darkness
To their stalls
Where they will spend the chilly night
Bedded in new straw
Listening to the quiet talk of owls,
And the midnight whisperings
Of tomorrow's tender grasses.

All day the cows

All day the cows
Stand in the field,
Their great bulk
Holding the ground in place
So it does not
Rise into the air
And drift away.

At night the cows
Return to the farmyard
And the barn,
And freed of all that weight
The pasture
Lifts gently off the earth
With a soft ripping sound
Like strips of velcro pulling apart,
Ascends in the moonlight
To hover above
The windbreak poplars
Beyond the fences,
And is blown about
Hither and yon
By the evening winds.

The cows sense
The pasture's departure
In the darkness
And murmur nervously
Amongst themselves
About what fate
May await them.
But by morning the field
Has settled back in
To its patch of landscape
As if it had never been gone,
The dewy grasses are fresh
And doubly delicious,
And the cows
Have become optimists again,

Happily grazing and gossiping
On a piece of ground
That might have landed anywhere
But wound up coming home.

Decline

At the ophthalmologist today
I learned that the macular degeneration
In my left eye
Bodes gnarly times ahead,
Although it is hard to say
How long before the condition
Begins to impair my vision.
The right eye right now
Is in a holding pattern.
The op doc and I will
Closely monitor the situation
In both eyes.
I will continue taking
My little red optical pills
And using my Amsler grid
To check for black holes.
In the meantime
I am enjoying the spectacle
Of highly disciplined straight lines
Breaking out of their rigid formations
And undulating sensuously
Right before my imperiled eyes.

My hearing aids are working beautifully.
I connect them each morning
To my phone,
Set the volume,
And go forth into the world
No longer listening to the ongoing goings-on
Through cotton balls.
From time to time during the day
I hear little chimes
In one ear or the other,
Something about incoming text messages
I presume,
Although I don't really know
And usually don't bother to look at my phone
To find out.
I imagine a guardian spirit

Ringing to check in
To make sure I'm still alive.
I should probably respond
And let her know
That my clock is still ticking
And that I enjoy her little tunes.

Recently we spent a few days
Up in the Sierra
At Royal Gorge near Donner Summit.
Cross-country ski trails
Make for great hiking when there is no snow.
We were going down one steep incline
When I slipped on gravel and fell—
But it was a soft spill, no harm done,
Because although they didn't keep me upright
My hiking poles interfered enough
With the gravity of the situation
To prevent me and my head
From slamming directly
Into one or another of the large boulders
Beside the trail,
Which could have accomplished
Some serious damage.
After the tumble
We continued to Long Lake
Where we sat on the shore for a couple of hours
Eating lunch,
Talking about our kids and grandkids
And where we would like them
To scatter our ashes.

I am grateful for the people
Who look after my various conditions
As I age
And grateful for the excellent gadgets and gizmos
I am able to use
To compensate for the sundry manifestations
Of my decline.

All in all
Still a wondrous life.

Somewhere near the Pleiades

When we die
And all our thoughts
Become suddenly
Unhoused,
Set free to wander aimlessly
All over the planet,
Probably all over the cosmos,
Will they grow morose
Being on their own
Without a cabeza full
Of other cerebrations
To interact with?
Will they become disheartened
When they encounter
The throngs of wandering cogitations
That have been left
With no fixed abode
And are knocking about
Looking for someone,
Anyone,
To listen to what they have to say?
Or will they after a time
Begin to fade,
To become hazy and translucent,
Unable to recall
Exactly what point it was
They meant to get across?
And will they find their way at last
To that friendly little tavern
Somewhere near the Pleiades
Where retired notions and concepts,
Ideas, fancies, speculations, hypotheses
Come together,
No longer trying to impress anyone
With how brilliant or insightful they are
But simply to enjoy
Each other's company,
Feeling quite relieved
That they have
Nothing left to prove?

Not to be confused with scribbling

for Freya

At the very beginning
Of the fifth century
T'ao Ch'ien decided to leave
The chaos of the capital
And go back to his home village.
Sixteen hundred years later
Our 3-year-old granddaughter
Decides that a map
Would be helpful for his journey
And draws one on the page
That contains the poem
Of his return.
The route is full of hazards and perils—
A long and winding road
Looping around towering mountain ranges,
Twisting through ancient forests,
Crossing over great river gorges,
Traversing trackless desert immensities—
But if followed carefully
It will bring T'ao Ch'ien to the terraced fields
He remembers so affectionately
And to the empty houses
Of old neighbors who have long since died.
He will grieve over the changes
Time has wrought
And brood about his own
Inevitable Great Transformation,
But will find that all he needs
To calm his fears
And bring his spirit back to life
Is to "let go and forget it all,"
With the help of a little spring wine,
While the diminutive cartographer,
Done with maps for now,
Moves on to her next project,
An exquisite portrait of herself
Sitting beside her kindly old grandpa
As he reads the poems of T'ao Ch'ien.

Reading to the dog

for Leona

I'm lying on the couch recovering from a cold
The little dog is at the other end so I can't stretch out my feet

Knees jutting upwards, I open a book of poems
And begin reading aloud so he can enjoy them too

He doesn't give any indication of listening
But you never know about dogs

We had a border collie once
Who was much smarter than we were

She might have appreciated poetry
But she was too busy rounding everybody up

I wouldn't even be surprised if dogs were poets themselves
With a venerable oral tradition

Perhaps our little terrier mutt is not howling at the neighbor's cat
But reciting lines he has composed himself

It's good to think of him as a writer of poetry
Which I could translate once I speak better dog

For now I'll keep on reading aloud to him
Hoping that a time will come

When the silver apples of the moon, the golden apples of the sun
Will make his tail wag wildly and his ears stand straight up

My new Swiss Army knife

Praise be to the goodly Swiss Army knife
For its uses are as numerous
As sparrows in a winter field.
For it cuts through apples and cheeses
And all manner of ropes and twines
And cardboard containers.
For it opens tins
And flicks off bottle caps.
For it screws and unscrews
In two languages,
Both Slotted and Phillips.
For it has a long blade and a short blade
Artfully shaped to points
Sharp with purpose and potential.
For it pierces leather
To create holes in belts and watchbands.
For it includes excellent scissors
Of unlimited possibility,
From snipping tags
Off newly-purchased clothing
To trimming the hair of old mens' ears.
For its tweezers remove splinters
And its toothpick supports dental hygiene.
For it boasts a well-tempered and sturdy utility hook
To hook utilities.
For its design is both pragmatic
And aesthetically pleasing.
For it shines like a ruby of great price.
For with this splendidly crafted tool
Tucked in my pocket
I am ready, willing, and able
To slice and dice,
To carve out a niche,
To cut the mustard.
For it is the gleaming realization
Of my boyhood cutlery dreams.

Beside themselves

In the large ceanothus out front
Entirely covered with small purple blossoms
And redolent with a beguiling fragrance
Of distant lilacs
The bees are beside themselves
Unable to pause
For the merest instant
As they pub-hop from flower to flower
To drink themselves silly
On the season's finest draughts.
And watching their boozy frenzy
I can't help but wonder
What it will be like in the hive
When they return home tonight.
Will each one grab a partner
To mazurka and jig and fandango
With utter abandon
Into the wee hours
While their patient queen mother
Oversees the wild goings-on
Smiling to herself
That bees will be bees?
Or filled with flagons
Of the joy juice of spring
Will they sink into sweet stupor
And dream of the siren ceanothus
With all her lascivious wiles and delights
Beckoning them
To buzz on over to her place for a drink or two
First thing in the morning?

What happened

We fell one day
Out of the sea
And said to ourselves
"What next?"
And since there was no answer
We started working on
Lungs and legs
And looking for a comfy little cottage
In Connecticut.
It was not easy
Living in the urgent flux
The place was overcrowded
And loud
You wouldn't believe the noise
Mostly from unruly procreation
And wild hunger
Not to mention
Rampant curiosity.
We had hordes of houseguests
But no one overstayed
And before we could say
Jack Robinson
Or Annie Oakley
We were frogs
Then turtles
Then just, well, bigness, largeness
Hugeness, enormity
Thundering daintily among
Forests and ferns
All over the map-less planet
Until some delinquent deity
Tossed a fiery chunk of universe
Into Chicxulub's kiddie pool
And oh, man,
The splash that launched
A thousand archipelagos
And an entire rethinking
Of the project
But not a newt to our name.

So, we rested then for a while
Trying to get our priorities straight
And maybe not as eager as before
To start dating again
Until one day
Along comes ice
Nice
And quiet
But don't let that fool you
It was remorselessly, stone-grindingly
Bone-bucklingly, mountain-pulverizingly
Canyon-carvingly
Funkily freezingly frigid
And what could we do but
Fur up
I mean huge hair all over our bodies
'Cause baby
Insulation was not on sale at Cave Depot.
So you had all these fuzzy brutes
Looking for cozy caves with a view
And maybe an in-law grotto and a kitchenette
Where they could spend a perpetual winter
Chewing each other to pieces
And by and by
Through no fault of their own
Voila! The ice changed its mind
And eased on out of town.
Minnesota found itself thoroughly lakéd
And everybody got a nice tan.
Not long after that
Agriculture
Enclosure of the commons
And the Roxy Ricochet Top 40
Featuring none other than the Duke,
Duke, Duke, Duke of Oil
With his Carboniferous Choraleers
Stinking up the joint and
Bunny-hopping us all
Back to the beach where we started

And where now we stand
Ankle deep in apocalypse
As the waters rise.

We do not identify flowers

We do not identify flowers
By color
Or the architecture of their blossoms
Or the medicinal properties
Of their roots and leaves and petals
But by the tiny songs they sing
When the wolves are out at night.

Thanksgiving Eve

Neatened up the Little Free Library.
Filled the neighborhood bowl
With water for passing dogs.
Made a cup of lemon ginger tea to sip
As I looked out the big front window
At the sunlight across the way
Being nudged ever higher into the treetops
By the shadow growing inexorably into night
As the air sharpened its frigid knives.
Thought about those with no home, no bed,
No place to escape the cold.
Wondered in what furious and infested alley
Justice will sleep tonight.

Another memorable performance

Whenever I get out of a chair
These days
I pause for a moment or two
To acknowledge the attention
Of the inner audience
Waiting breathlessly
To see if my various joints
Will successfully execute
The complex maneuver
Necessary to take me
From sitting to standing
Without a catastrophic collapse
And when it becomes clear
That I have delivered
Another memorable performance
Then, modestly, I nod and wave
As I swan along the boulevards
To wild applause

My 80th spring

Old watering can filled with rain.
Blueberry plants loaded
With tiny bell-shaped blossoms.
Weathered wood-slat fence
Threatening collapse.

First day of my 80th spring.
The winter has been wild
With storm after catastrophic storm
Bringing hillsides to their knees,
Causing roads to cave in on themselves,
Houses to slide into the ocean.
And meteorologists tell us
We're not done yet.
But no rain today
When my wife and I walk in the watershed
With two granddaughters,
Hunting for wildflowers,
With scant success
Because we need a few more sunny days
To bring out the poppies, the lupine,
The sticky monkey and hound's tongue
And wild irises,
In all their vibrant colors.

My 80th spring.
Not hobbling exactly,
But slow and cautious
Going up and down
The muddy hillside trails,
Stepping over fallen trees,
Crossing swollen creeks,
Which I can no longer
Confidently accomplish
Without the aid
Of my indispensable hiking poles.

Eighty spring times.
Who knows how many more?

I never imagined I'd be this old,
Older than my father,
Older than Tu Fu and T'ao Ch'ien,
Older than memory.

Vernal equinox of my 80th year.
Wooden fence leaning precariously.
Blueberry plants flowering in profusion.
Banged-up old watering can filled with rain.

About me

for Nina

About me
My granddaughter explained to a friend,
He's a good guy
But he's really slow.
For obvious reasons
I tingle with pride
At the first half of that assessment
Because I can think
Of no higher praise.
Regarding the second half, well
I cannot deny its veracity.
The arthritis gnawing
At my joints
Has considerably diminished
The velocity
Of my comings and goings
Making me less useful
For certain tasks; for instance
You wouldn't want to have me
Walk to the local ice cream joint
For a quart
Of vanilla honey lavender
Because by the time I got home
It would be more cream
Than ice.
If there's no hurry, however
I'm the fellow you can
Send to the market
For a loaf of bread
A jar of pickles
A bunch of bananas
A dozen eggs
A bag of flour—
You-name-it.
I've got a sturdy staff
To help me remain plumb,
And for hauling cargo,

A durable old daypack
That I've carried for decades of hiking
In mountains and deserts and forests.
So as long as there's no need
For speed
I can still deliver the goods.

#2 pencil

(a little Pablo Neruda, a little Christopher Smart)

Praise be for the #2 pencil
For it is the perfect object
Of simplicity and utility
For it is elegantly slender
With faultless posture
For it contains all words
For it is equipped to eliminate its mistakes
And start anew
For it is inexpensive and thus
Available to all
For its weight is not so great
That it tires the hand
For its weight is not so slight
That the hand drifts off the page
And loses track of where it is
For it does what is asked of it
And makes no comment
On the tasks it is called upon
To perform
For when its lead breaks or wears down
It is submitted to sharp blades
Of various types
And does not complain
For it perceives itself
Growing smaller and smaller
And understands its own mortality
Yet it does not grieve
Does not shirk its duties
For it understands its role
In the scheme of things
And carries on without a whimper
For even when it is reduced
To little more than an eraserless nub
It will write one more grocery list
Draw one more map
On a napkin
Jot one more telephone number

On a torn envelope
Before it is tossed for good
Into the trash bin
Where it will rest in peace
Having lived a life
Of selfless service
To all the jotters and doodlers
All the underliners and notationists and figurers
All the scorers and sketchers and puzzlers
Of scribbling, scrawling humankind

Mail

The tattoo on my soul reads
Return to sender
But I'm guessing I'll probably end up
In the Dead Letter Office

If I were in charge

If I were in charge,
The moon would be so bright
On warm summer nights
That birds could not sleep
But would instead pass the hours
In uproarious vocalizing
So loud it would wake
The whole neighborhood.
But instead of annoyed or angry
The neighbors would be thrilled
By the unexpected oratorio,
Would put on slippers and robes,
Would make cups of tea
And go out to the front porch
To sit and listen to the jubilant counterpoint
Of warbles and chirps and tweets.
If I were in charge,
After a long mellifluous night
Of unexpected song
The moon would grow pale
As it drifted downwards
Toward the horizon,
And the newly wakened sun
Would begin performing its diurnal duties
Even as the birds kept up
Their melodious hullabaloo
And the day broke wide open
Like a glittering piñata.
If I were in charge.

After a long pause

for Walt, Clara, Rod, Barb

We're practicing insomniacs
With tricky knees and creaky backs

In various stages of disrepair
Arthritis here and cancer there

Our hearing's headed slowly south
And now and then we lose a tooth

A page of print is faint and blurry
And why are kids in such a hurry?

You'd think we'd sink into the blues
With all our plaints and lousy news

But here we are, by luck, or grace,
Once more meeting face to face

Strolling under turning leaves
Recalling other days like these

And all the moments, all the years
We've jumbled into memory's drawers

Like flannel shirts and old wool socks
That keep us warm on autumn walks

As friendship, too, has kept us warm
Through decades come and decades gone

Now past becomes our present tense
As old friends gather once again

Winter night

Winter night
Full moon walking the streets
Peering through the windows
Of the fortunate
Who lie warm in their beds
While the heartsick footsore homeless
Slump in doorways
Huddle under bridges
Crawl into cardboard boxes
And the hard frost to come
Waits like a panther in the treetops
Clicking its bone cold teeth

A day in November

The light today
Is the brightest kid in class
The kid who knows
All the answers
The kid who raises a hand
Even before the teacher
Asks the question

The light today
Is everybody's best friend
Dishing out compliments
Like shiny new dimes—
"Your whole face glows when you smile!"
"Sparks fly off you when you dance!"
"That picture you painted is radiant!"

The light today
Hangs by its knees
On the monkey bars
Kicks the ball a mile
Dazzles while jumping rope
Runs the bases
In a flash

The light today
Plays all the glistening instruments
In the band
Writes its name
On easels and chalk boards
Lies in little golden patches
On bookcases and desks
Whispers to the most studious
To look up from their work
For a moment or two
And gaze out the window
At the gloriously hued leaves
The glinting azure sky
The lengthening afternoon shadows
The sun drifting slowly westward

And light itself growing ethereally pale
Getting ready to settle in
For the long night
After another scintillating day
Of being the star pupil.

Falling down in five chapters

    Chapter 1. Quick recovery

In the first millisecond
Of your sudden descent
You believe
That you can still right yourself
And carry on as you were,
Making your way down the stream bank
Before your untimely misstep.

    Chapter 2. Calculating options

When you realize
That a quick recovery of vertical counterpoise
Is not a viable possibility
You consider various alternatives
For effecting a safe landing, e.g.
Curling into a ball,
Covering your head with your arms,
Twisting your body somehow
To re-aim it
At that patch of mud
And away from the large rock
That is glowering at you
From the terminus of your trajectory.

    Chapter 3. Surrendering to reality

It soon becomes clear to you
That a body in freefall
Has limited options,
"Oh, fuck,"
You explain to yourself
Just before your corpus and the Earth
Encounter each other
In what could not be described
As a tender embrace.

Chapter 4. Assessment

You lie perfectly still
On the wet, stony ground
Noticing that your glasses
Were smart enough
To abandon your face before impact
And are lying in a puddle
Close to your left ear,
Apparently undamaged.
Good for them.
Your wife rushes to your side
And requests a quick self-triage.
Everything hurts a little,
Nothing hurts a lot.
You stand up slowly
And find you are able
To continue on your way
Around the lake,
Limping only slightly,
While you monitor your interior workings
For any malfunctions,
Any new pangs and throbs.

Chapter 5. Aftermath

Back at home
You call the advice nurse
Who reads off a list of symptoms:
Dizziness, severe headache, nausea,
Blood or other fluids
Pouring out of your cranial orifices.
No, no, no, and no, you reply,
Relieved that one more time
You seem to have escaped serious injury
And wondering if this may have been
Your last free pass.

Coda

Next morning
You wake up hurting
In no place in particular
But everywhere in general.
You feel a kind of exhausted aching
Of the soul,
And are deeply pessimistic
About your chances of landing that job
With Cirque du Soleil.

Gray, somber day

Gray, somber day
Cold, wet air
Sparrows and juncos
Pecking half-heartedly
At the muddy ground
As if they couldn't care less
The woods drained
Of all color, except,
High up on a tree
Standing beside the fire road,
Amongst a profusion of leaves
Dead but not yet fallen,
A single, tiny, ripe persimmon
Hollering its prayer
At the top of its wee little voice—
ORANGE! ORANGE! ORANGE!

The Cote d'Azur

You would not believe
How much time I spend every day
Getting older.
A rough estimate:
100% of my waking and sleeping hours.
Fortunately, I have found ways
Of fitting other endeavors
Into the small cracks
Between episodes of decline.
I manage to read a good book now and then
To take a fine walk in the hills
To play silly games with our granddaughters
And when I do that
I experience a momentary rush of optimism
As everything seems to be going along
Swimmingly—
Bodily deterioration on hold
Mental acuity in peak condition
Reflexes sharp
Pains subsiding in every precinct.
But alas, it is a fleeting instant
Of false hope
For after a bad night's sleep
Aging reappears
In all it's fanged ferocity
Like a steroidal neo-colonialist
Intent upon re-occupying my body and mind
Subduing my spirit
Multiplying my miseries
And reminding me that this bus
Goes in only one direction,
And while it may wind me through
Some gorgeous countryside
With spectacular scenery
I am fully aware
Of its final destination—
And it ain't the Cote d'Azur.

Merit badges

(21 merit badges are required to become an Eagle scout)

What I loved most
About being a Boy Scout
Were the accoutrements—
The olive-green uniforms,
The colorful patches and pins,
The yellow kerchief,
The garrison hat
Tucked smartly under
My adjustable belt
With the shiny brass buckle,
The pocket knife, the compass,
The canteen,
The right-angle flashlight.
Attired and equipped with it all
I became an apprentice hero,
A John Wayne in the making.

Now that I'm an old man
The appurtenances
Are considerably different—
Hearing aids,
A dental bridge,
Fusty old cardigans,
A walking stick,
A back brace—
Decking me out
And gearing me up
For the ordinary heroics
Of an elder fellow's daily life.

I was a lousy Boy Scout.
And, although I learned
To tie a bowline around my waist
With one hand,
To camp in the snow
Without expiring of cold,
To tap out messages

In Morse code,
I didn't earn a single merit badge,
And I picked and chose
From the famous list
Of Boy Scout virtues—
Obedient didn't make the cut.

But these days
I am taking my Senior Scouting
Very seriously,
Being sure I keep up
The daily maintenance
Of all my hardware
While earning one merit badge after another—
Medication Monitoring,
Car Key Retention,
Bladder Discipline,
Heel-First Walking,
Prescription Decoding,
Jar-Lid Opening,
Goofing with Grandkids,
Giving No Advice,
Backing Up in Parking Lots,
To mention just a few—
And chances are good that I'll be an Eagle
When I finally fly away.

Clouds of memory

Could it be
That the white puffy clouds
We love to watch
Drifting and shifting
In the amiable atmosphere
Of a warm day in summer
Or a brisk autumn afternoon
Are actually memories
That have escaped,
Or been evicted,
From the noggins that housed them,
And are now free to wander
The great wide sky
Without any compulsion
To be home and available
For nostalgic conversations
About the good old days,
For disagreements about who
Set Aunt Eugenie's hat on fire
Or who broke Grandfather's crystal snifter?

Will the clouds stay aloft,
And slowly fill with moisture
Which will rain down
Upon the earth?
Will all those memories
Be absorbed by soil,
Swell streams and rivers,
Carry nutrients to forests
And prairie grasses?
Will they slake our thirst
With someone else's amazing journeys,
Someone else's first love?

Old poets

Talking on the phone
With an old poet friend of mine
Who's wondering if anybody
Will want to read his new poems
About being an old poet.
Who would have any interest
In an octogenarian versifier's
Encounters with decrepitude?
Maybe other geriatric cases,
He says,
But they already have plenty of first-hand information
About the topic.
He's right, of course,
Who, no matter what age,
Wants to read about someone's
"Plights & gripes
As bad as Achilles"?
Younger people aren't eager to envision
What might be coming their way,
And oldsters
Probably won't be captivated
By an exquisite metaphor
For incontinence,
A lyrical description
Of an arthritis flareup,
An unforgettable portrayal of memory loss,
Because, well,
That's all too close to the bone.

Many years ago a well-known poet
Whose body was slowly heading south
Wrote a book of poems
About his experiences
Of advancing old age.
The writing was frank
Unadorned, intensely personal,
And when I finished reading it
I wanted to fling the damn thing
Across the room

Because with each poem
All I could do was picture myself
In the disheartening circumstances
He described.

So what's the solution for my friend?
I will tell him to send the poems to me
Because he's a good writer,
A good compadre,
And I'm happy to be an audience for him,
But I will prepare myself
To be sad,
Not for him in particular
But for all of us on board the midnight jitney
Headed for the last stanza,
The poignant final image,
The end of the line.

Life is different in your eighties

Life is different in your eighties.
When you phone an old friend repeatedly and no one answers
Your first thought is not
"She must have gone out for the day."

Life is different in your eighties.
When you have a sudden crick in your neck
Your first thought is not
"Oh, it will work itself out."

Life is different in your eighties.
When you forget the name of book or a movie,
Your first thought is not
"No worries. The title will come to me."

Life is different in your eighties.
You can tip over just standing still
Looking up into the trees for the hawk's nest
Or the branch where the purple finch is singing its heart out.

Life is different in your eighties.
When your little granddaughter asks if you're going to die
You answer her with your *second* thought—
"Not for a long, long time."

Life is different in your eighties.
The unexpected does not surprise,
So much that mattered so much matters little,
The commonplace shines and shines.

Masterpiece

I did not make this day
But I would be happy
To take credit for it.
The catalog entry will read:
Wednesday, March 8, 2023/
Mixed media/
By Buff Whitman-Bradley.
Although nothing of any historical significance
Occurred on that day
It is memorable for
Its reverberatingly brilliant blue sky
And the cold air
Freshly scrubbed by weeks of rain
That caused many people
To pause and remark
What a thrill it was
To take a breath.
It was a day when patches of mud
On forest trails
Were as glossy and slick
As black ice,
When throngs of ever-hungry crows
And sparrows and towhees
Scavenged the ground
For morsels newly unearthed
By the recent rains.
It was a day in which everyone felt kindly
Toward everyone else,
And patient,
And generous,
And forgiving…

All kidding aside,
It took an entire cosmos
Billions of years
To assemble the myriad parts and pieces
Of this magnificent day,
And although I do not belong
To the culture crowd,

I do recognize a masterpiece
When I am walking around in one,
And that's what today is.

Sadness

Your sadness
Is your oldest friend.
It accompanies you everywhere
But does not call attention
To itself.
Like a sweet old mutt
It just tags along
Because it does not want
To be all alone
And lonely,
It does not want you
To be all alone
And lonely.
It stays off to the side,
Or discretely behind you,
In the half-light,
Out of the way,
Not expecting or demanding
Your constant attention,
Content to be quietly nearby
When you are occupied
With some important task,
Or spending time
In the company of others.

On your walks in the woods
Your sadness trots along beside you
In the tall grasses,
And sometimes
When you stop beside a creek
Or sit down on a log
Your sadness nuzzles up so close to you
You can feel its breath
On your face,
You can hear
The pulsing of its blood.
The tenderness
Could break your heart.

Something wonderful

Let's not talk any more
About all our aches and pains,
All our afflictions,
All the portents of doom
Haunting the corridors
Inside our creaky old bodies.
Instead let's talk about
The day's first cup of coffee,
Beautiful bicycles glistening in the rain,
Where we're going to walk
When the weather turns fair.
Let's talk about
What a surprise it is
To still be alive at our age,
What a delight it is
To hike in the woods
And see a varied thrush,
A pair of baby owls,
A bobcat padding nonchalantly
Through the brush of a hillside clearing.
It is growing late.
Join me. Sit here.
Tell me something wonderful.

Your name

for Rod Anderson

If you lead an exemplary life
And play your cards right
A distant galaxy
May name one of its constellations
After you,
Or a great river
May bestow your name
On one of the streams
That form its headwaters.
When this happens
Your entire life will be
Exactly as it was before.
Astronauts will not map
Interstellar journeys
Using your name as a reference point,
Grammar school children will not
Read your name in their geography books.
And when you die
Your passing will not be noted
By anyone other than those
Who knew you
When you were not yet a flashing rivulet,
A grouping of stars,
And who will miss your presence
Because of how graciously
You flowed among us,
How unfailingly you shone.

After his funeral

for Barb Anderson

After his funeral
When the large vases of flowers
Have been distributed
To various family members and friends,
When the platters of homemade cookies
And brownies and lemon bars and poundcake
Have been emptied and wiped clean,
When the coffee urn has been rinsed out
And returned to its cupboard,
When the photo boards have been packed
Into the backseats and trunks
Of his grown children's cars,
When the songs his grandchildren sang
In delicate and tearful harmonies
Are quietly repeating themselves
In the inner ears of departing mourners,
Then the family goes back to the home
Where they often came together
When he was alive,
To sing and grieve
And laugh and weep
And stitch a counterpane of memories and stories
That will cover them all,
To finish the heaps of food
Neighbors have been dropping off every day,
Stuffing themselves silly
With casseroles and lasagnas and baked beans
Until all the empty plates and bowls
Are piled high in the sink,
Stomachs are full
Broken hearts grow drowsy,
And grief rolls up her sleeves
To wash the dishes
And straighten up the house.

Just now an ant

Just now an ant
Was making its way
Down my computer screen
Minding its own business
Doing me no harm,
Probably heading home
After a hard day at the office,
And without thinking
I reached up
And brushed it off
Sending it hurtling down
Toward the floor.
I immediately felt guilty
And I wondered why I had committed
That small, thoughtless act of inhospitality.
Small to me, of course,
But imagine the ant
Strolling quietly down the screen
Maybe humming a little tune to itself
Or wondering what's for dinner
When some cosmic cataclysm
Comes upon it
And overwhelms its entire existence
Flinging it into space
To land somewhere
Far from where it had been
And far from where
It was intending to go.
Imagine the ant
Utterly bewildered
By the mysterious forces
On the loose in the universe,
Forces that seem to have no regard
For the health and well-being of an ant,
Forces that hurl it willy-nilly
Into emptiness
Not caring whether it lives
Or dies.
I am so sorry, little ant.

You and I inhabit the same indifferent universe
And we both could use
All the comfort we can get.
If you ever make it back this way
Rest assured that I will not
Swipe you off my computer screen again,
That I will offer you
Sympathy and support
As you travel
Toward your destination,
That I will acknowledge and appreciate
All we have in common
As fellow beings doing our best
To make it to the checkered flag
In one piece.

ACKNOWLEDGMENTS

With thanks to the following publications in which the poems noted first appeared.

American Journal of Poetry: "#2 pencil"
Comstock Review: "We do not identify flowers"
Coneflower Café; "Tomorrow's grasses"
Dissident Voice: "Somewhere near the Pleiades," "Thanksgiving Eve," "What happened"
Evening Street Review: "After a long pause"
Fleas on the Dog: "A bit plonky," "A day in November," "Another memorable performance," "Beside themselves," "COVID booster," "Winter solstice"
Front Range Review: "All day the cows"
Glacial Hills Review: "The Big Tomato," "Bishop Woodpecker," "Growing old"
Main Street Rag: "Sadness"
New Verse News: "Goodnight Earth"
Pinyon: "Heat wave"
Poetry Pacific: "All will be well"
Rushing Through the Dark: "About me," "Almost out loud," "Clouds of memory," "Old poets," "Roadside grasses," "Summer jobs"
samfiftyfour: "Morning hawk"
Steam Ticket: "Frog songs"
Third Wednesday: "Ants," "Cote d'Azur," "Falling down in 5 chapters," "Just now an ant," "My 80th spring," "Three hawks," "Your name"
Third Act Poems (podcast): "After his funeral," "Birthday poem," "The blackberries of August," "A cold, gray day," "Decline," "Existential blues," "Lucky stars"

Buff Whitman-Bradley has been writing poetry for sixty years now. This is his sixth published book of poems. In addition, he has written two nonfiction books for middle school readers, and a handbook of poetry-related language activities for teachers to use in the classroom. In the early 2000's he was a member of the organizing collective for Courage to Resist, and created the Courage to Resist Podcast, for which he interviewed members of the military who refused to fight in Iraq and Afghanistan. He and Sarah Lazare and Cynthia Whitman-Bradley turned those interviews into the oral history book *About Face: Military Resisters Turn Against War* (PM Press). He taught school for 15 years, including nine in kindergarten. He also worked in publishing as both a writer and an editor, for *Sunset* magazine, *Learning* and *Family Learning* magazines, and *Parenting* magazine, and received professional commendations from the Educational Press Association and the International Reading Association. He podcasts his poems at thirdactpoems.com. He and his wife, Cynthia, live in northern California.